Wild Spirit

By

Neethu Padikkoth Rayaroth

FanatiXx Publication
ISO 9001:2015 CERTIFIED

FanatiXx Publication

AM/56, Basanti Colony, Rourkela 769012, Odisha

ISO 9001:2015 CERTIFIED

Website: *www.fanatixxpublication.com*

© Copyright, 2023, Neethu Padikkoth Rayaroth

"Wild Spirit"
By: Neethu Padikkoth Rayaroth
ISBN: 978-93-5605-109-6
English Poems & Quotes 1st Edition
Cover Design: Sagar Samal
Price: 199.00 INR
Printed and Typeset by: BooksClub.in

Dedicated to all my family members and loved ones who provided me a constant support and encouragement in completing my book.

About the Author

Neethu Padikkoth Rayaroth is a native of Kerala, an IT professional working in Bangalore who loves writing articles and poems on life, love and all that are part of modern world and our existence. She is more interested in chess, music, and debates on different outlooks of world occurrences and most importantly has a zeal to bring the change. On most occasions, she writes poems to express the wild imaginations in her thought process. She believes in women rights and strives for women empowerment through her writing. Her goal is to voice out for the change in society on the perspective towards women and bring in gender equality for the upcoming generations.

Connect with her via Instagram: @inquisitive.thoughts , Facebook: Neethu Padikkoth

Acknowledgment

A lot of hard work, effort and time spent in writing this book. To create a coherent sequence was a challenging experience and the chapters that I have created in my imagination, I am glad it turned out the way it is supposed to be. Most importantly, I experienced a great deal of learning in this journey and a creation of pathway for me to travel in my writing journey. So, an acknowledgement to myself for believing in me and my strengths.

A special thanks to my husband 'Rohit Samly' for the constant support in everything I do, his encouragement to write this book and for being a part of my life. The constructive feedback he provided upon proof-reading and those honest opinions have immensely helped me to evolve this book into its finest version. I am also thankful to my family members and friends who believed in what I do and what my capabilities are and their encouragement to write this book.

Lastly, Thanks to 'FanatiXx Publication' and the team for helping me in publishing this book and being part of every step of this publishing journey and all the hard work that is being put to make this into a reality.

Preface

This book 'Wild Spirit' consists of three different chapters. **'Pursuit'**, **'Grief'** and **'Revelation'**. Each chapter depicts the pathways we choose for ourselves in the journey of life. I have written *'Pursuit'* with an objective to bring readers the simple nuances of life we grow up watching, experiencing, loving, and living in the moments. Yet nothing in life stays forever. The more we grow old, the more we forget the simple pleasures that makes the life in its finest form. Pursuit becomes a dream in our memories when the obstacles creeps in and that's what the chapter *'Grief'* represents - The depth of mixed emotions we experience when life gets complicated.

Is Grief more of an illusion from our end? Could there be an alternative outlook to our life than *'Pursuit'* and *'Grief'*? Given a chance, would you look beyond these simple nuances and hurdles with an alternate perspective? Would that change the way you navigate through your life? Indeed, that's what the last chapter is all about. I have written the chapter *'Revelation'* to showcase readers that life is and never was all about what *'Pursuit'* or *'Grief'* teach us. There is more to living if only you care to look for.

I would humbly request all my readers to not just read along, but to experience the scenery as we move along the flow of poetry one after the other. In the end, the intention is to bring out the readers the takeaways of *'Revelation'*. If I succeed a little in my attempt, I strongly believe that you would realize how there are different outlooks and infinite possibilities for the events in life and all it takes is for us to look beyond and seek out the light in our existence.

Pursuit

JUST
Breath
~ FLORA ~

Let's start simple. Shall we?
A book by your side, hot coffee in hand and
staring out the window.
Those droplets of rain dripping through the leaf.
Peace Indeed!
A sense of ease softens your mind.

What's more worthy than a life living in the moment?

That was simple pleasure indeed. Isn't it?
Perceiving the nature as it blooms. How about you live it a little more?

Standing in the balcony.
Sharing the moonlight
and earphones,
humming to the beats of
our favorite songs.
With love, we share
countless old memories
and laugh it off with
champagne glasses.

Ah, the moonlight. No words could describe the charm of its radiance. In all those countless moments, did you ever stare right through the sky and wondered what we know of the beauty it beholds?

Z
Z
Z
Z

On star-gazed summer nights,
the moon smiled ever so bright.
Pastels of little starts painted the night sky
and vast blue curtain speckled in moonlight.

Oh, she glowed ever so white!
The night flowers watched in awe
and coral reefs danced in love,
ever so softly, twinkled in her shine.

Well, sky is the limit they say. Have you ever wondered about the limits of Ocean?

Sand dunes and beach on a Sunday evening.
That smell of the sea and the tides calling.
I want to lay down under the palm trees
and embrace the spirit of being alive.

In reality, all of us have admired the beauty of the sky, the ocean, the rain, the wind and the moonlight. In fact, everything of the universe we live, we watched in awe as we grew up. Yet did you ever explore the aura of the nature by experiencing it in the simplest of actions that you perform in life?
Shall we explore them as we read along the next poetry?

Up in the woods, those winter mornings
where fog covers up and you watch the
mist lay out its soft blanket,
you slowly hum the words of magic
and hope for the winds to swirl them and
resonate around the corners.
You dream of the rain that tastes like
melody on your lips and fade along your skin.
Those intense moments, you witness the
light thrive and grow in your heart
slowly snugging you with a white quilt.
Indeed, you surrender yourself to this calmness.

Calmness – They say, the state or quality of being free from strong emotions.

You see, often we crave for something that is non-essential to us, yet we ignore the simplest flavors the world could offer us. Like the calmness in nature, we pay no attention to, in the midst of rush. In the next poetry, would you for a moment pause the rush in you and engage yourself with the nature?

Your footprints pressed hard in soil
that smells of warmth and embrace.
Gathered winds ruffle around your skin.
Withering autumn leaves fall off
in peace; a rhythm of gusting winds.
Your eyes twinkled bright
as the orange hues gloom
and spiral in hustle.
You lay down over the patches.
A blanket rich of gold and red fallen petals.
The sunrays slowly make its way
between the spaces,
for a soft fall into your soul.
A reminder of your promise to live kind.

Now, would you walk a little more, ponder a little more of all that you see and experience?
What did you find out of all this? Let's read along the final piece that gives away the takings of this chapter.

A lingering kiss of the sunset.
Whispers of leaves in hustle.
Cold winds and sweet musings.
On days like this, calm and serene,
I would sit by the lemon tree
with silent wish to drink the moonlight.
To cross across the seas and mountains
and watch all that is infinitely beautiful!
Ah, my dreams don't have boundaries.

Yes, our dreams don't have boundaries. Should you desire, you may cross the seas and mountains and reach the stars, only if you could pause your rush for a moment and look around. Alas, isn't it unfortunate that we don't just stroll around life that way? Life gives us diverse seasons to traverse through, yet we are stuck in trivial despairs of life.

Let's contemplate in the next chapter '*Grief*' on how we crumble at the feet of complications in life, eventually slipping away from the memories filled in chapter 'Pursuit'.

Grief

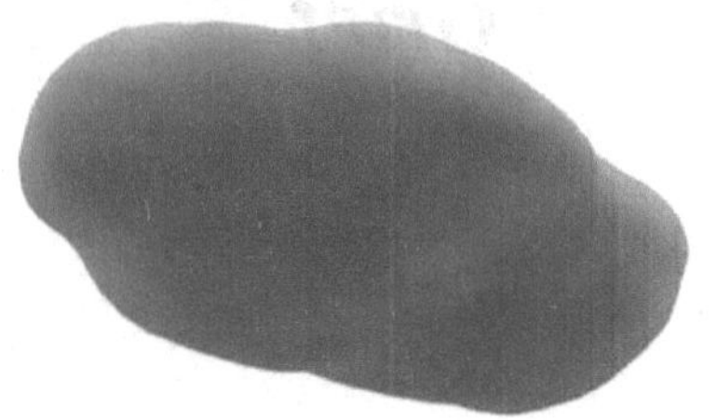

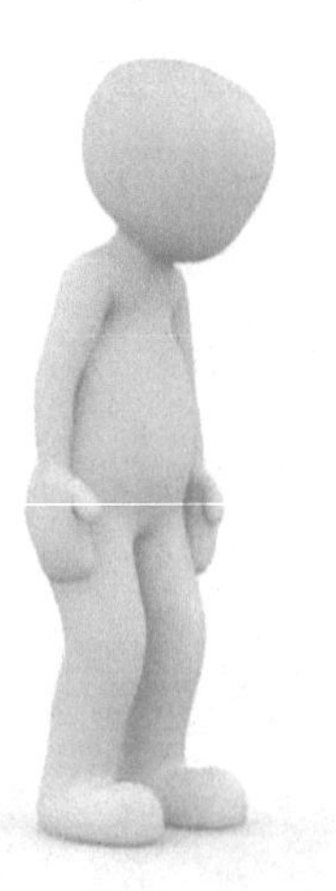

In the course of life, most of us restrict ourselves from true happiness by raising the bar of our desires. At every instance of success, we hope for more and more until our energy drains out and the reality hits. All desires are not meant to be achieved. The greatest acceptance in living is the acceptance to let go of things that are not meant for you and to be truly grateful with the blessings that you receive.

If you are one such human who run behind the success over success, the chapter '*Grief*' is for you to ponder.

In this Chapter, I would like to take the readers through the stages of emotions humans go through. Just remember to scenarize them as you read along.

The Denial

When desires don't bear fruit, would you choose to let them go? or would you be someone that holds on to them until it hurts? This piece is to that denial, to that disagreement in you to let go what's not meant for you.

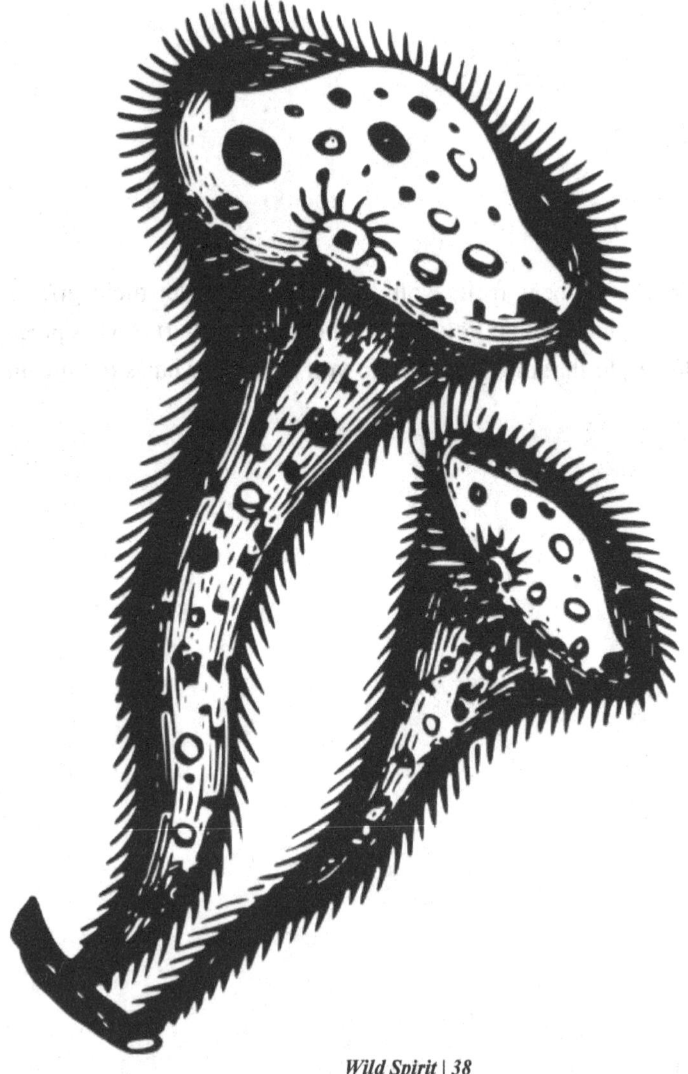

First, it seemed like shallow water
with beautiful coral reefs and
luminous fishes swimming around.
I let my leg slip a little by little
wondering how far I could go.
Little did I know,
in the whimsical charm of desires,
I have gone too deep inside.
Holding onto them in vain,
I scream with all my strength.
Only when desires turn rusted
in the grasp of deep-water algae I realized,
Only when those scars etched in my skin
and nothingness washed over me I realized,
I could have let them go and set myself free!

The Despair

People tend to lose hope in their living at the instance they lose something they love or fail at the feat of something that is built for years.
The following piece depicts the emotional loss of affection that a human craves for. Despite investing yourselves emotionally, sometimes people lose the care of their dear ones merely because their affection lack empathy you expect.

Fleeting between the boundaries
are the agony and despair,
mourning the loss of affection.
What is valued and not valued?
What is affection without empathy?
Drowning in the teardrops
are the hopes to heal!
To reconcile and regain,
yet dissolving into the ocean
of sorrows and pain.
A resignation to the inevitable loss.

The Depression

A resignation to the inevitable loss.
You see, often people with soft heart and kind soul are the weakest. The one who struggles in conquering failures and subsequently a slow leap into depression. It's inevitable indeed. It's a slow death. But have you ever talked about your grief to someone? Have you ever questioned your self-existence?

If you are that someone who is fortunate enough to not go into depression, this piece should give you the idea of a depressed person. And, if you are that someone who goes through depression, this piece is to let you know that people do understand. Your hope is never lost, if only you could hold on a little longer.

You cry, scream and try to explain all in vain.
All that is just reflected as sadness to them.
How do you explain to them it's not?
How do you explain that you go through this
overwhelming emotions for no reason at all?
A ghastly swamp within you, an agony
sulking you into the maze of madness.
How you wish you could look at their helpless eyes
and tell them that you tried and tried and tried
picking up all the broken pieces
to fix them and stay alive?
But you failed!
You can't fix it. Can you?
How could you if you don't know
what is broken inside?
Paranoid of irreparable damage,
the night comes again and again,
so are your nightmares.

The Agony

The next piece is for the pain within you.

I have written this piece to give out my best in unraveling the pain we hold somewhere deep in our heart. Some people hold onto them more, some ignore them and some of us don't realize but we all have a suffering deep inside our heart. In fact, some people go through pain, unspoken and unexpressed.

I churn the moulds of my brittle bones
to heal in the midst of falling.

Hollow and brutal veins.
Bruises ache where the lights trace.
I grapple with the flesh of my skin
withering chaos and mourn.

I try peeling off layer by layer
to slip away all the wounds I own.
Exquisite thread of pain weaved in soul
gather around, coming undone,
falling off the edges in fragile.

Perhaps, we all yearn the silver lining
to be raw and warm
 in our life afloat,
amid the darkness we hold.

The Grief

Speaking of pain comes the grief -a mourning to the loss of something or someone dearer to us. An overwhelming emotion. To be able to cope with grief, to move past the loss is a gradual acceptance to the new beginnings of life.

This piece is in the view of a grieving person falling off the edges to death amidst the fantasy of falling in love.

I fall through the dark,
miles and miles of vast space.
Hard and fast.
Flares of skin
breaks apart.
One after the other,
my collapsed veins
and cracked bones
shatter across.
I sprint down hard in
broken pieces
but the falling didn't hurt.
For I become nothing
but a mere soul falling
to rest in your safe arms.

A Slow Death of Irony...

In her stillness, there is a pounding heart.
Emotions that are huge to be felt.
It aches for an embrace, a warmth
and intense desire to acquire.
The pulsating heart; a slow fallen silence.
An epitome of memories.
Too pure to be hurt.

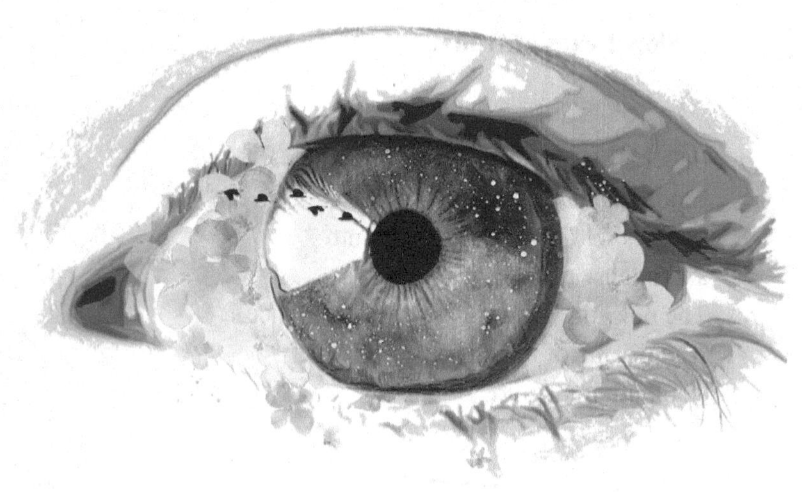

The denial, despair, depression, agony and grief are the major stages of emotions humans experience in their life, mostly out of the decisions they take. However, at many circumstances, it's not the grief or depression or failures that crumbles a human. It is the world that you receive and give to others. Don't we all move in a fast-pacing world with lack of morals and empathy in our heart?
Aren't these stages of emotions a mere part of our actions to each other?

A final piece to showcase the readers, the kind of world we live and offer to the future humankind.

We live in the world
that wear attires of gold
 and satin shimmering on the skin
yet the insides drowning in
rusted iron of dirt and narcissism.
How long are we this way?
Ever-changing world full of humans!
Automated bots of loathing
and self-pleasured beings.

Our morals turn grim,
thinning at the borderline
desperately feeding kindness
to our cold hearts.
We let the world turn grey,
manifesting worms of self-love
and less compassion.

Oh dear us, wake up or
the days aren't far indeed
to be engulfed by our exploding filth.

I would like to end this section 'Grief' with a reminder to all of us. To slow down, pause and refresh life with more of compassion and less of ego.

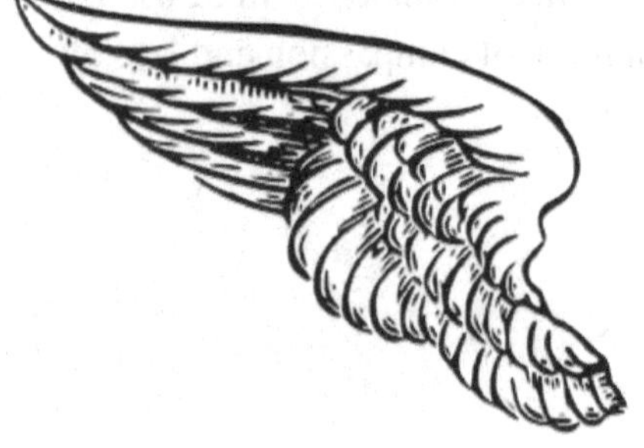

Revelation

So, we have gone through '*Pursuit*' and '*Grief*' and if you are with me all along imagining out each poetry as we read through, then my heartfelt Thank You for your effort. I hope I have managed to give you some insights on how we started perceiving our life as we born and how we perceived life as the tide changes and the darkness lurked in.

I would request you all to hold onto it a little more and read along my last and favorite chapter 'Revelation'.

So, you learn from mistakes they say. There are endless possibilities and outcomes for every decision we take in our life, yet we always perceive the outcomes that bring us grief. With the chapter 'Revelation', I intent to bring you the readers the alternate possibilities that help us look beyond and appreciate what life offers us in abundance.

Hope this chapter gives you the revelation of life as much as I have experienced.

First on a positive note,

Remember, your story is still unfolding.
Embrace the scars like a warrior.
Best is yet to come!

We often lust over the luxurious things in life, a craze for the indefinite possessions, a materialistic addiction and all things that are extraordinary in our ordinary life. We never think of contentment or a gratitude towards what we receive. Yet when our hairs turn grey and death knocks at our door, a tiny part of our heart realizes where true peace lies in.

In the truest simplest forms of life, isn't peace is what we all crave for?

In life,
all that you need is a sense of being alive,
breathing through a peaceful heart.
To love and to be loved.
To care and to be cared for.
All that ever mattered is a simple contended spirit
as light as a feather in a misty air.

As much as you want your life to be a feather in a misty air, have you ever looked into the beauty of scars in the middle of your remarkable life?

In the midst of colors,
would you still find Grayscale beautiful?

To begin with, let's start teaching ourselves the art of self-love. One poetry at a time! Shall we?

A Reminder to Your Heart from Yourself

We are all in this together.
Hoping,
Healing and
Recovering.

Self – Acceptance

You are as beautiful as the universe
with a palette of magic in your heart.

Self-Confidence

Darkened skies and shattered dreams
yet my self-reflection under moonlight
spoke of all the ways I healed.

Self-Affirmation

You are that gorgeous chaos
molded in ball of fire.
You wore pride as an armor
and conquered kindness in heart.
You are that unapologetic soul,
unguarded and fearless.
Oh, you do taste like wine
dripping magic from your skin.
Perhaps, demons burnt in flames
when you breathed
dreams into life.

Self-Courage

Don't be afraid to fly high,
even if you must crash-land.
What matters the most is,
you never gave up on your dreams.

Self-Love

The night sky taught me
silence is beautiful!
So are the moon and stars
whispered quietly
to glow in silence.

And I glowed!
Like a stardust
full of magic and fire.

Self-Assurance

With the sunrise
is the moment that softens
all the aching and tears.
Golden rays that grow
wildflowers in dark corners.
You are to bloom again,
beautiful and reckless.

Self-Appreciation

Gorgeous are those
vibrant eyes and revered smile.
You are that beautiful soul
made of primroses and diamonds.

Self-Belief

If it has to be a fall,
I would fall gracefully
till the demons
in my bones
shatter and scream
and crumble at my feet.

Self-Motivation

Let that series of mistakes
break you a little.
Let the grief go cold
and shiver your spine.

Chances are your finest act
and wildest dreams
come alive at your vulnerable most.

Self-Rewarding

Fill that heart of yours
with all that is magical and light.
Like fireflies and crescent moon.
Like raindrops on rose petals.

Self-Admiration

We are all poems,
poems waiting to be undone.

We are born of soft heart and indigo eyes,
yet we spend days in war with ourselves.

More often than not, we see the colour of our soul
wanting to spill and dance in curiosity.

Why deny it – the world,
when the world has so much to offer?

Tomorrow when you watch the morning rise,
let your spirit dress up gracefully yet slowly
in all its madness and freedom.

Now, the true art of '*self-care*' lies within the art of exploring one's inner self.

Before we move onto the next piece, would you take a moment to think about the mysteries hidden behind your ravishing soul? How so wonderful it is to explore the marvelous magic our spirit possesses within? Would you explore the spirit of your own soul as you read along the next piece?

This is my art. This is what I believe of my soul and I hope you would believe the same of yours.

The Art of Exploring Myself

You are free to explore me!
Unravel the mysteries
of my fearless soul.
You will find the magic
come alive in my sensuality.
A mad rush of love
oozing through my skin.
Should you decide to stroll beyond,
you will find the adventures
of my dreams,
a bit of wilderness
and soft mellows
flourishing at the corners.
Oh, I tell you.
You will be mesmerized
to walk eternally in the
universe of my spirit.

Now a Pause. A Refresh to a Beautiful New Start

Given a chance
to freeze this moment
and suspend the time we spent,
I would undo all that rush
I carried through my life.
I would let the life flow
in its way, one moment at a time.
A well-spent, well-lived memories
and most of all,
an abundant space in heart
for beautiful new dreams.

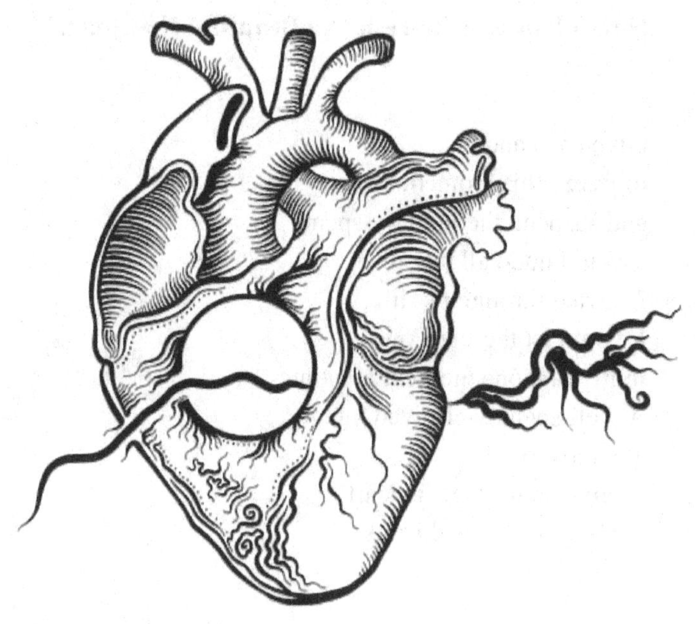

And Now for the New Growth

Somewhere I read,
"I am 75.
Closer to the end than the beginning."

For some reason, it stuck my heart.
How so much of life is left, yet
we are stuck in the past!

Do wildflowers need consent to bloom
or the rivers need approval to flow?
Why the humans seek validation to grow?

The colors of your heart don't
have to be graceful for the
wonders in you to thrive wild.

To Love and To Be Loved

You are meant to be loved,
by someone like winter sun.
You watch their warmth
melting in your bones.

You summon to the foreplay
of their tenderness.
You surrender to their
soft soul spreading on your lips.

Why to be enough?
when you could starve
and awaken by their storm?

Why to survive?
when you could learn
the art of living in their madness?

It is beautiful! Isn't it?
To be undone in the edges of the unknown.
To be wholesome in the laughter of love.

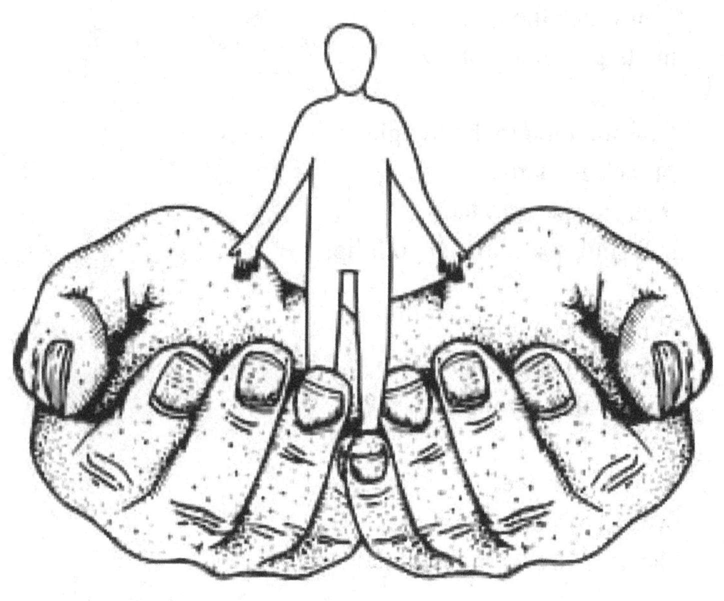

To Be Wholesome

Feed your heart the affirmation
of love; of belonging.
Carry the flames in your spirit
like the fervor of restless tides.
Remember you are offering this world
your wholesome and tenderness
as you sow kindness in your heart.

To That Peace Within You

Until the wilderness in eyes fade
and our withering bones perish,
endless miles we run
leaving dreams at footprints.
A rush in wild race
manifesting pride and greed.

For once, would we wish to pause,
turn around and inhale.
May the immense tranquility
in all its glory yield our heart
with life of abundance.

To Be Aware of Little Things

Sometimes a familiar warmth; a familiar smile.
Be interested in simple things.
An elusive little things.
You know those things that make you aware of
fleeting memories and pensive dreams?
Yes, that's what am talking about.

To That Spirit Within You

Never let your scars choose your boundaries.
You are to live life in abundance.

To Your Vulnerability

All the rawness and mess.
This vulnerability and bruises.
You are made of many-layered textures.
You can be the light for one day
and bite back on the next.
You are allowed to feel not guilty
for choosing path for yourself.

To The True Believer in You

Some people run and run
until they wind up in circles.
Some people are just dreamers
living in painted dreams.
Some would just whisper words
dunked in tasteless honeycomb.
Yet you go for the light
to reach that extra mile,
to taste that fresh air,
to crawl out of the darkness,
to be naked without ugly ideals.
You are the true warrior
born with the womb of earth
and mountain of dreams.
Your stories would unfold the poem
your children grow up to read.

Finally, A Promise to Yourself

This burning inside of you.
Keep Breathing.
A fall won't hurt, I promise.

And most importantly, something that you give.

Kindness – The most inexpensive gift one could give

Love them the hardest.
The one who seek for the soul
beneath your skin.
The one who bleed kindness
for your broken heart and
the one who embrace your scars
as much as your smile.

Now, a final piece dedicated for all my readers and the loved ones who spent their precious moments of their time to read and support me in this journey.

This is for That Wilderness in Your Heart

Live a little foreplay of your dreams.
There is always a new beginning
to life and all the moments you wasted.
Flirt recklessly with your soul
until a warm smile gathers around your lips.
Laugh a little.
Cry a little.
Let there be a growing space to heal.
But most of all,
Remember to live and not exist.

Lastly, A Special Piece to Myself and for My Book

You know those lilac flowers.
The one that blooms soft and small.
My poetries are like them.
It could be soft; it could be delicate.
But those are mine.
Unscathed and deep.

I often tremble at the thought of being naked,
of rawness these words unravel.
Perhaps, we expose a little of us and
discover a little of ourselves in poetry.

Dear readers, if you have reached till this point and managed to read my poetries, I am indeed grateful to you for your incredible effort and interest in reading my book.
I hope I have managed to take you through the various aspects of life and different perspectives we choose for ourselves. Let there be revelation in you to choose the best outcomes in your journey.

Wishing you all the success and wonderful life ahead!

You can contact the Publisher at:
www.fanatixxpublication.com